It's the middle of the night and
the snow has started to fall.
Color in the snowflakes with lots
of bright colors.

# My Big Book of CHRISTMAS Activities

## Make & Color Decorations, Creative Crafts, and More!

### Clare Beaton

FOR YOUNG READERS

Racehorse for Young Readers books may be purchased in bulk at special discounts for sales promotion, corporate gifts, fund-raising, or educational purposes. Special editions can also be created to specifications. For details, contact the Special Sales Department, Racehorse for Young Readers, 307 West 36th Street, 11th Floor, New York, NY 10018 or info@skyhorsepublishing.com.

Racehorse Publishing ™ is a pending trademark of Skyhorse Publishing, Inc.®, a Delaware corporation.

Visit our website at www.skyhorsepublishing.com.

10 9 8 7 6 5 4 3 2 1

Library of Congress Cataloging-in-Publication Data is available on file.

Design: Louise Millar
Editorial: Catherine Bruzzone and Sam Hutchinson
Production: Madeleine Ehm
Cover design by Louise Millar
Cover artwork by Clare Beaton

Print ISBN: 978-1-63158-415-2
Ebook ISBN: 978-1-63158-423-7

Printed in China

# In this book

From party hats to Advent Calendars, there are plenty of festive projects in this book to help you prepare for Christmas. If you want to skip straight to the cards, gifts or decorations, then page numbers are below.

You will find festive templates at the front and back of the book and on pages 13 (stocking), 22 (triangle), 27 (gift pouch), 52 (various), 61 (cone), 62 (napkin ring).

Before you start on a project, make sure you read it through and get everything you need ready. Work on a clean, flat surface with plenty of room. If you need to use scissors, knives, the iron, or the oven, be careful and have an adult standing by.

The ♻ symbol has been included throughout the book to show where you could use recycled materials. Here below are some of the essential things that you will need, some of which can be recycled.

★ plain paper or light card ♻
★ colored and patterned papers ♻
★ tissue paper and gift wrap ♻

★ sequins, foil, and glitter ♻
★ pencil and ruler
★ scissors and craft knife
★ glue and sticky tape

★ tracing paper
★ crayons, paints, and felt-tip pens
★ thread, yarn, and string ♻

**Take care when using a craft knife.**

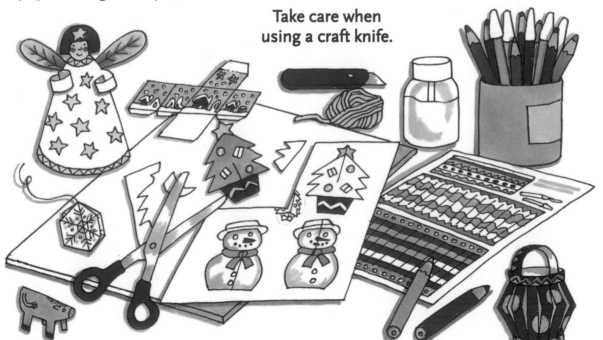

# How to use templates

If you need to use any of the templates at the front and back of the book, here is how to do it very simply and successfully.

*What you will need:*
★ tracing paper ♻
★ soft pencil ♻
★ sticky tape
★ paper

Trace the template shape with the pencil. Tape down the tracing paper to keep it still.

Turn over the tracing paper and scribble over the lines with the soft pencil

Turn over again and tape on to the card paper. Retrace firmly over the lines. Remove the tracing paper.

# Christmas Fun

## How it all began

Christmas is the festival when Christians celebrate the birth of Jesus. Jesus was born in a stable over 2000 years ago in Bethlehem, which is now in Israel.

Many of the things that are popular at Christmas date back to the story of Jesus's birth: star decorations represent the star the three kings or wise men followed to the stable; and the giving of presents began with the gifts of gold, frankincense, and myrrh that they brought to baby Jesus.

Christmas greenery dates from before Jesus's birth. Ancient Druids and Romans used to decorate their houses with evergreen branches for their important winter festival, the Winter Solstice.

Christians all around the world celebrate Christmas on December 25th. In some countries, ike Australia and Argentina, Christmas is in the height of summer.

# Christmas Customs

Here are some of the many ways countries
all around the world celebrate Christmas.

## St. Nicholas, Santa Claus, and Father Christmas

These are just some of the names for the
"gift bearers". In Holland, Austria, Belgium,
Switzerland and parts of Germany, December 6th is
St. Nicholas Day when children receive presents.
In Britain, America and Australia, December 25th
is the day when children wake up to find their
stockings have been filled with small gifts
by Santa Claus or Father Christmas.

## Christmas Cards

Christmas cards were
invented in England, in 1843,
by a man called Sir Henry Cole.
Millions of cards are now sent
worldwide and many charities
raise money by selling them.

## Christmas trees

They were first enjoyed
in Germany but now people in many
countries have a decorated fir tree
as part of their Christmas celebrations.
Holly, ivy, and mistletoe are also popular.
It's bad luck to leave decorations up
after January 6th!

## Christmas Crib

The nativity scene appears in all churches and also in many people's homes. In Germany there are Christmas markets every winter selling figures and cribs.

## Christmas food

Every country has its own special festive cakes, biscuits, and breads of every flavour and shape. Biscuits are hung on the tree in Scandinavia and Germany. In Britain and America, turkey is the most popular choice for Christmas dinner, while beef is the favorite in Italy and pork is eaten in Greece. In countries where Christmas is in the middle of summer, Christmas dinner is often a barbecue on the beach.

## Christmas Carols

Carols, songs about the birth of Jesus, have traditionally been sung by groups of people collecting money from door to door. Carol concerts are always very popular at Christmas time.

## Crackers

Christmas crackers were invented in England in 1847 by Tom Smith. They are great fun for the Christmas table and are popular worldwide.

# Festive Pom-poms

*What you will need:*

* thin card
* pair of compasses
* pencil
* ruler

* scissors
* ¼ yard of net fabric
* 11 in length of yarn
* glue
* glitter

1

Draw a circle, 1 inch across, on the card. Use the same center point to draw another circle measuring 3 inches across.

2

Cut out the ring and make a second one by drawing around the first. Place them together.

3

Cut strips 3/4 inch wide.

Cut the net into strips. Using two strips at a time, wind the net around the rings until the central hole is almost filled in.

4

Push the yarn between the rings and tie in a knot. Tear off the card rings.

Push the point of the scissors between the net and two card rings. Cut the net around the rings.

These gorgeous pom-poms are made in the same way as yarn ones. Hang them in a row along a shelf or spray them silver or white to hang on a Christmas tree!

Hold the pom-pom firmly by the yarn and dab the edges of the net with glue. Roll the pom-pom in glitter. Use one color or mix two together.

Net comes in lots of wonderful colors. You can use two or three colors at the same time. Make cool frosty pom-poms in mauves, white and blues, or rich red, green ones.

# Tree Cakes

*What you will need to make 14 cakes:*

* ½ cup softened butter
* ½ cup caster sugar
* 2 eggs
* ½ cup sifted self-raising flour

* chocolate finger biscuits or chocolate flakes or liquorice sticks
* cake decorations and small sweets

1

Beat the butter and sugar together in a bowl until pale, light, and fluffy. Add the eggs, one at a time, with a tablespoon of flour.

2

Smooth the top with a knife.

Carefully fold in the remaining flour with a metal spoon. Put into a rectangular 7 ½ in x 11 ½ in cake tin.

3

Cool on rack and ice when cold.

Cook in the center of the oven at 350°F for 25 minutes. Leave in the tin for 5 minutes. Cut into triangles.

## Butter cream icing

½ cup softened butter
1 cup sifted icing sugar
1 tablespoon milk
few drops green food coloring

1 Beat the butter until it is soft.
2 Gradually beat in the sugar and milk.
3 Keep beating until it is light and fluffy.
4 Add the food coloring.

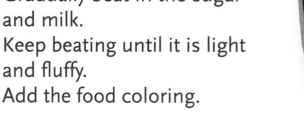

These cakes look quite spectacular with their green icing and colorful decorations. Serve them on a board with a spatula and plenty of napkins for sticky fingers!

Cut up chocolate finger biscuits, chocolate flakes, or liquorice to make tree trunks. Push them into the bottom of the cakes.

Make each cake different with lots of cake decorations and small sweets.

11

# Christmas stocking

*What you will need:*

- ★ pencil and tracing paper
- ★ 16 ½ in x 19 in piece of felt
- ★ pins
- ★ scissors
- ★ small pieces of felt for decorations
- ★ colored threads and needle
- ★ yarn
- ★ darning needle
- ★ beads and sequins

**1** Cut two stocking shapes.

Using the adjacent stocking template and instructions on p4, trace the shape on to tracing paper. Pin on to the felt.

**2** Add decorations to one side only of each stocking shape.

Use the templates at the front to cut decoration shapes out of felt. Pin and sew them on to stocking shapes. Decorate.

**3** Don't sew the top.

Pin the two stocking shapes together and sew around the edge with colored yarn and the darning needle.

**4**

Cut a felt rectangle 4 ¾ in x ¾ in. Fold it in half and sew to the back of the stocking at the top using yarn.

Make a stocking in red or green felt or use different colors each side. Sew on red beads for holly berries and add sparkly sequins to stars.

STOCKING TEMPLATE

Use colored threads or yarn for sewing on decorations and for extra details.

# snowflakes

*What you will need:*

- ★ pair of compasses
- ★ pencil
- ★ white paper
- ★ scissors
- ★ glue
- ★ glitter

Draw a circle 6 in in diameter on the paper. Cut it out and fold it in half. Fold one third over.

Fold the other side over the top. Cut a V shape in the center of the folded paper. Cut more shapes along the folded edges.

Carefully dab glue over the snowflake and sprinkle glitter all over it. Shake off any excess.

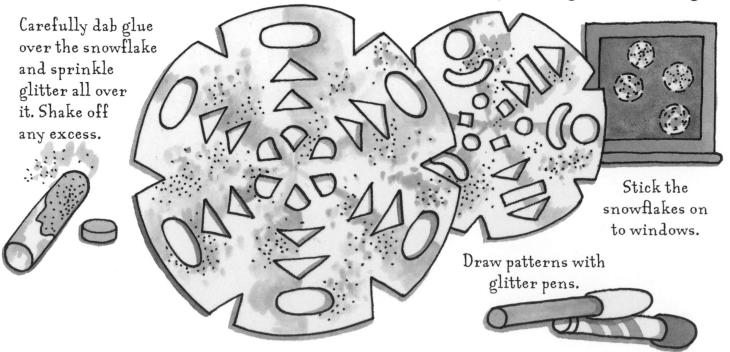

Stick the snowflakes on to windows.

Draw patterns with glitter pens.

# Christingle

*What you will need:*

- ★ orange, candle
- ★ raisins
- ★ 4 cocktail sticks
- ★ red ribbon
- ★ pin
- ★ sharp knife
- ★ saucer

A "Christingle" means a Christ-light and they are made as part of a festival held on December 13th to remember the bravery of a young girl many years ago. St. Lucia risked her life in Sicily taking food to fellow Christians who were not allowed by the Romans to follow their religion.

**what the christingle represents:**
Orange – the world
Candle – Jesus, the light of the world
Red band – the blood of Christ, shed for the world
4 sticks – the four seasons
Raisins – the fruits of the world

Ask an adult to help light the candle.

1  Ask an adult to help you.

Push the candle into the orange.

Make a hole in the top of the orange big enough to hold the candle. Fasten the ribbon around the orange with the pin.

2

Spear several raisins on the cocktail sticks and stick them into the orange. Place the orange on the saucer.

# Christmas Cards

## DOVE card

*What you will need:*

* ★ 4 in x 12 in colored paper
* ★ pencil and tracing paper
* ★ white paper
* ★ scissors
* ★ black pen
* ★ glue
* ★ sticky stars

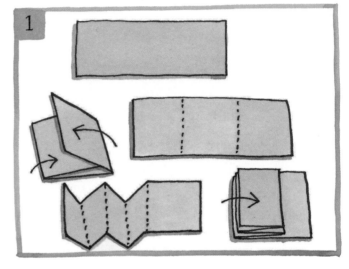

**1**

Fold the colored paper into three. Open and fold two of the thirds into two so they are like a concertina.

**2**

Draw on eyes with black pen.

Using the instructions on page 4 and the dove template at the back of the book, trace and cut out three white paper doves.

**3**

Glue the top two doves so that the heads and chest stick out.

Glue each one a little higher than the other.

Stick on star.

Glue one dove at the bottom of the right-hand third of the card. Glue each of the others on to the folds above it.

Here are two very different cards to make for your friends and family. Write your message on the back of the dove card, and inside the star card.

## star card

*What you will need:*

★ colored paper (as big as you like)
★ different-colored tissue paper
★ scissors
★ glue
★ sticky stars or sequins

**1** Fold the colored paper in two. Cut small squares of tissue paper. Glue them on to the front of the card.

**2** Stick the stars in the center of each square. You could glue sequins here instead.

# Advent Calendar

*What you will need:*

- ★ 2 sheets of white paper measuring 11 x 17 in each
- ★ pencil
- ★ felt-tip pens or paints and paintbrush
- ★ scissors
- ★ 1 piece of colored paper measuring 11 x 17 in
- ★ glue
- ★ craft knife

Draw 24 buildings on one of the white pieces of paper. Draw a window or door in each. Make a large one for day 24.

Cut out the buildings. Arrange and glue them on the colored paper. Cut out the windows and doors on three sides.

Place the colored paper on the other white sheet. Open the flaps. Draw the door and window shapes on the white paper.

Draw pictures inside these boxes. Put glue around the outside of them. Press the colored paper down over the top.

You can make this Christmas village as decorative as you like—add patterns on the roofs and walls. Draw trees, bushes, snowflakes, stars, etc.

Make sparkly snow with glue and glitter over the roofs.

Use small metallic shapes for decoration.

# Festive Wreath

*What you will need:*

★ wire coathanger
★ greenery such as ivy, holly, and fir
★ ornaments
★ plastic-covered plastic bag ties
★ ribbon

Bend the coathanger into a circle. Wind ivy round and round the wire.

Add pieces of holly and fir. Fasten them with the bag ties. Keep adding them all the way round.

Use ties to fasten the ornaments on to the wreath. Space them evenly apart.

Make sure ornaments and leaves are facing the front. Fill any gaps. Tie a bow at the top and hang it up.

Hang this festive wreath on your door as the Christmas holiday approaches. Create your own special one using whatever you can find.

If you can't find fresh greenery then you could use plastic instead.

Use other colorful decorations if you prefer them to ornaments.

# Christmas Circles

*What you will need:*

- ★ old Christmas cards with the backs cut off
- ★ pair of compasses
- ★ pencil and tracing paper
- ★ scissors
- ★ glue
- ★ paperclips
- ★ yarn
- ★ sticky tape

**Triangle template**

Trace this triangle on to a card. Cut it out

**1** Draw ten circles, 3 ⅛ in across, on the old cards. Cut them out. Using the triangle template, draw a triangle on each circle.

**2** Put paperclips on the glued sides while they dry.

Bend the circles along the straight lines with the colored sides upwards. Glue five curved segments together to form a "flower" shape.

Make a second "flower" in the same way. Tape the end of some yarn on the plain side.

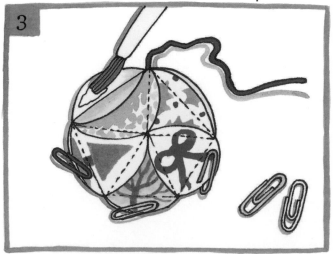

**3** Glue the two "flowers" together on the remaining curved segments. Put paperclips on these while they dry.

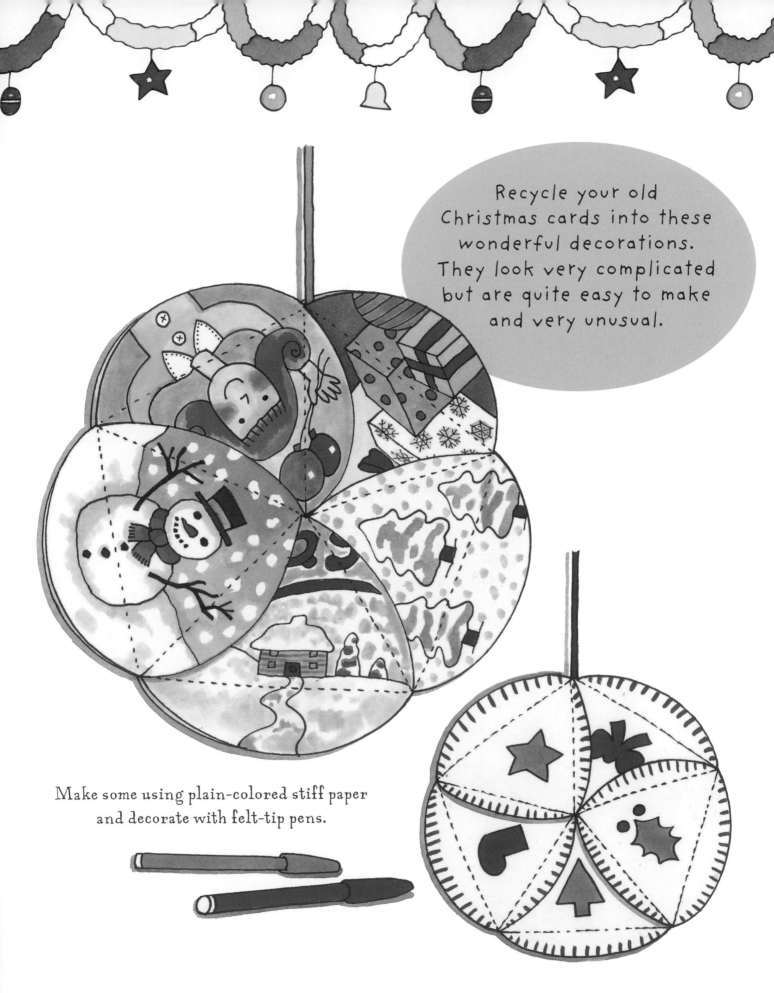

Recycle your old Christmas cards into these wonderful decorations. They look very complicated but are quite easy to make and very unusual.

Make some using plain-colored stiff paper and decorate with felt-tip pens.

# Nutty Nougat

*What you will need:*

- ★ ½ cup toasted almonds
- ★ ½ cup toasted hazelnuts
- ★ 2 large egg whites
- ★ 4 tablespoons runny honey
- ★ ½ cup caster sugar
- ★ rice paper

**1**

Ask an adult to help you chop the nuts. Beat the egg whites until they are stiff. Mix the nuts into them.

**2**

Put the honey and sugar in a small saucepan. With adult help, bring it to the boil. Stir it from time to time.

**3**

Remove the pan from the heat and add the nut mixture. Return to a very low heat and cook for 8 minutes, stirring occasionally.

**4**

Place weights on the paper and leave to set for 24 hours.

Line the bottom of a shallow plastic container with the rice paper. Pour in the mixture and press it down. Cover with rice paper.

When the nougat is set, turn it out on to a chopping board. Cut it into small squares.

Once it is wrapped, this nougat will keep for a few weeks. If you put it in a pretty box or bag it makes a lovely Christmas present.

Cover the nougat in foil and add star stickers.

Wrap in colored cellophane and twist the ends together.

Nut allergy
WARNING!

25

# Gift Pouch

*What you will need:*

- ★ 7 in x 9 in stiff colored card
- ★ pencil and tracing paper
- ★ scissors
- ★ craft knife
- ★ glue
- ★ paints and paintbrush
- ★ glitter

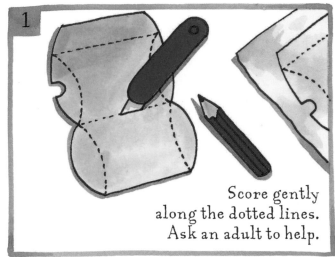

**1**

Score gently
along the dotted lines.
Ask an adult to help.

Using the instructions on page 4
and the template opposite, trace the
pouch on to the card. Cut it out.

**2**

Paint decorations.

Draw shapes, add glue
and shake over glitter.

Decorate both halves, except the flaps.
Follow the instructions on page 4
to trace the template shapes.

**3**

Fold flaps with
'bites' last.

Fold the pouch in two. Put glue on the
big flap and stick it under the opposite
side. Fold in the flaps at either end.

These clever boxes make the perfect way to wrap small gifts. Use contrasting colored tissue inside.

## POUCH TEMPLATE

Glue this flap.

Use colored corrugated card.

Try different colors—even the printed side of a cereal packet.

Make a gift tag and tie it on. Use the templates at the front of the book and the tracing instructions on page 4.

# Christmas Jokes

* What is Tarzan's favorite Christmas song?

Jungle Bells.

* Why did the turkey cross the road?

To prove he wasn't chicken.

* Who is never hungry at Christmas?

The turkey—he's always stuffed.

*What do cannibals eat for Christmas dinner?

Baked beings.

* What is the wettest animal?

A rain-deer.

*Who gets the sack on Christmas Eve?

Father Christmas.

# Ho! Ho!

# Pocket Money Christmas

In this section, you will find lots of lovely projects for festive gifts, cards, and decorations. They do not cost much to make and many of them use materials that you might have thrown away. Your pocket money will not only go a long way, but you will also help the planet.

Have a look at pages 30-31 to see all the kinds of things you can keep to recycle. Old clothes, plastic bags, and candy wrappers are not rubbish at all!

The symbol ♻ in the list of things for each project shows you where you can use them. There are template shapes on page 52 and at the front and back of the book. See page 4 for how to trace from a template.

Here's a guide to the star system used for each project:

★      very easy and quick.

★★     will take a bit longer.

★★★ more of a challenge.

# Treasure not Rubbish

Here is a selection of things you can keep to use for the projects in this book and for others too.

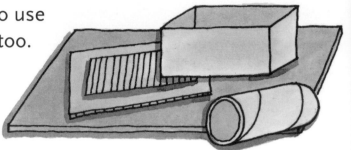

## Old Wool Clothes

Put old sweaters and other woollen clothing into the washing machine on the hottest wash. This will shrink them and produce a "felty" effect.

## Card, Cardboard Boxes, and Tubes

Small, large, thick, thin, and corrugated are all useful.

## Plastic Bags

Keep thicker, colored ones. It doesn't matter if there is writing or pictures on them.

## Candy Wrappers

Keep jewel-colored foils and cellophane.

## Old Jeans

Wash them. It doesn't matter if they have some holes!

## Scraps of Material

## Giftwrap, Tissue Paper, and Greetings cards

Save old paper and smooth it flat with a cool iron. Keep it flat or roll it up. Save old greetings cards you like.

## Large Plastic Bottles

Wash and remove any labels. See-through and colored bottles are both useful.

## Corks and Metal Tops

Rinse bottle tops and dry them.

## Buttons

Every color and size.

## Wire coat Hangers

## Twigs, pine cones, and Shells

While on walks in the countryside, park, or on the beach, pick up interesting natural objects.

# Party Hats

Make these with your friends for a party or make some for each of the family to wear at the Christmas dinner.

 ## Crown

- ★ thick, colored paper ♻
- ★ candy wrappers ♻
- ★ scissors
- ★ ruler and pencil
- ★ glue
- ★ sticky tape or stapler

Cut strips of paper 4 in wide and 23 in long.
Draw and cut a pattern along one side.

Pull the strip into a circle.
Tape or staple the ends together.

Glue on crumpled candy wrappers to decorate.

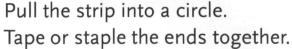

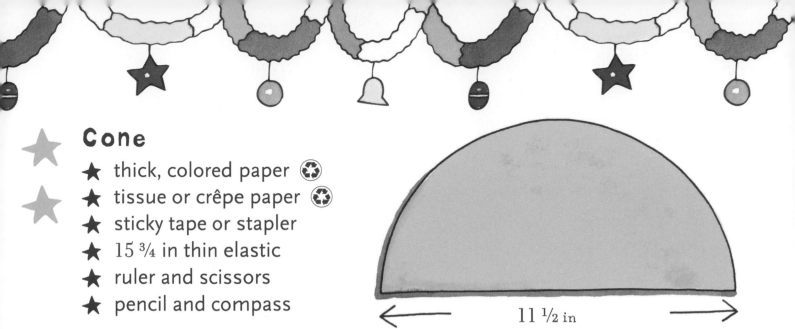

## ★ Cone

- ★ thick, colored paper ♻
- ★ tissue or crêpe paper ♻
- ★ sticky tape or stapler
- ★ 15 ¾ in thin elastic
- ★ ruler and scissors
- ★ pencil and compass

← 11 ½ in →

Draw and cut out a semi-circle of paper.

Pull the paper round to form a cone. Secure with sticky tape.

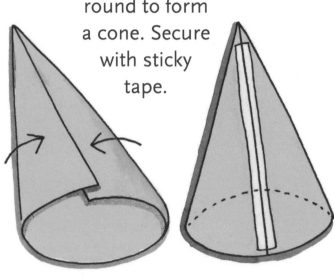

Cut some tissue or crêpe paper into a 5-in wide strip. Cut it into a fringe.

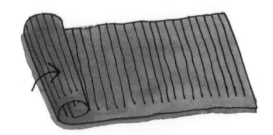

Cut a tiny bit off the point of the cone. Roll up the fringe and poke the uncut end inside the cone. Secure inside with tape.

Cut some narrower fringes. Roll them up and attach them to the cone with sticky tape or a staple.

Tape the elastic inside. Wear with the elastic on the back of your head. Make the elastic longer if you want it to go under your chin.

Ruffle them with your fingers.

33

## Pillbox Hat

- ★ thick paper ♻
- ★ crêpe and tissue paper ♻
- ★ sticky tape or stapler
- ★ glue and scissors
- ★ 15 ¾ in thin elastic
- ★ 2 rubber bands

Cut a strip of thick paper
2 ½ in wide and 19 in long.

Join the ends with sticky tape or the
stapler to form a ring.

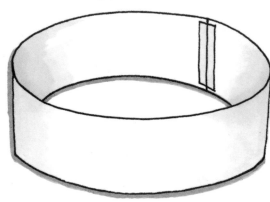

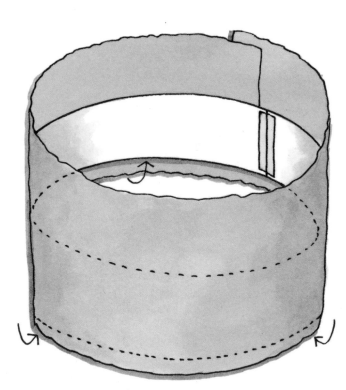

Cut the crêpe paper into a strip
8 ¼ in wide and 20 in long.
Glue this strip around the paper ring.

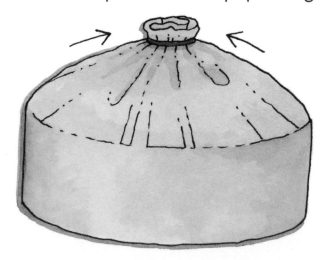

At the bottom, turn the crêpe paper
a little up inside.

Draw the crêpe paper together in the
center and secure with a rubber band.

Cut different-colored tissue paper into small fringes. Wind them around the gathered crêpe paper and attach them with the other rubberband. Fluff them out.

Attach the thin elastic to the inside of the hat. Wear with the elastic on the back of your head. Make the elastic longer if you want it to go under your chin.

## Christmas cake Hat

★ white crêpe paper ♻
★ giftwrap ♻

Make this like the Pillbox Hat but when you gather the paper into the center on top, tape it flat.

Cut a strip of giftwrap the same size as the ring. Cut the long edges into fringes and tape around the ring.

Cut out the Christmas templates with flaps from page 52. Color in and stick them on top.

# Decorations

## Paper chains

★ giftwrap
★ ruler and scissors
★ glue

Cut the giftwrap into strips
1 in wide and 8 ¾ in long.

Put glue on one end of the strip. Form
into a loop and glue to the other end.

Loop a second strip into the first
and glue the ends together.

Carry on in this way to make a long chain.
Make lots and hang them up.

## Christmas Tree Baskets

★ stiff colored paper ♻
★ patterned paper ♻
★ glue and sticky tape
★ pencil and compass
★ ruler and scissors
★ wrapped sweets

Draw and cut out one circle of plain paper 1 ½ in in diameter and one a little smaller of patterned paper. Glue them together.

Cut a strip of colored paper ½ in wide and 8 in long.

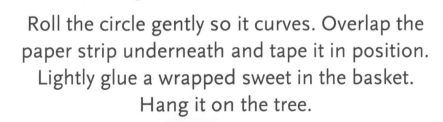

Roll the circle gently so it curves. Overlap the paper strip underneath and tape it in position. Lightly glue a wrapped sweet in the basket. Hang it on the tree.

### Variations

Cut the circles with pinking shears.
Cut the circle edges into small fringes.

## Fan Garlands

★ tissue paper in two colors ♻
★ ruler and scissors
★ glue
★ stapler or sticky tape

Cut the tissue paper into strips
1 ½ inches wide and 4 ¾ in long.

Fold into a ¾-in
wide concertina.
Secure one end
with a stapler or
sticky tape.

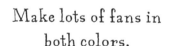

Make lots of fans in
both colors.

Stick the fans together
by gluing them along
the outside edge.

Join each fan,
alternating the colors,
and with the ends
alternating up and
down.

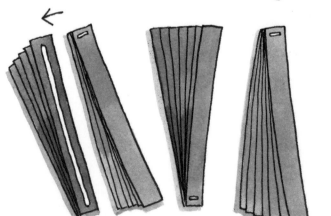

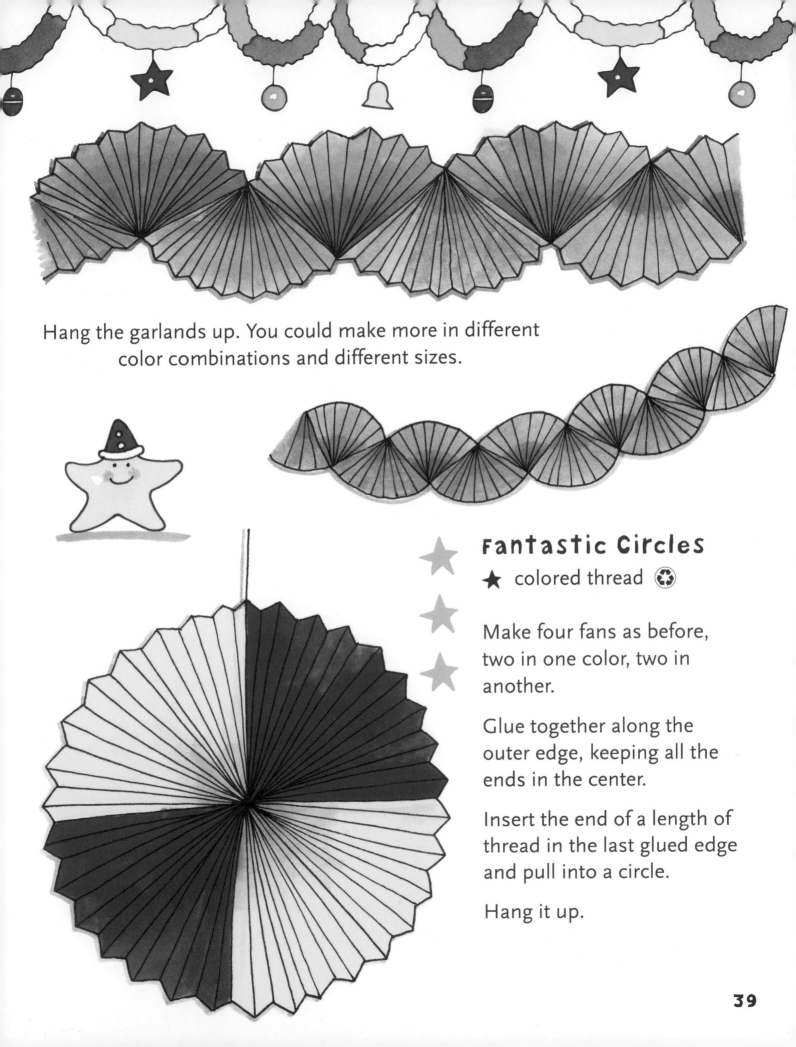

Hang the garlands up. You could make more in different color combinations and different sizes.

## Fantastic Circles

★ colored thread ♻

Make four fans as before, two in one color, two in another.

Glue together along the outer edge, keeping all the ends in the center.

Insert the end of a length of thread in the last glued edge and pull into a circle.

Hang it up.

# Festive Food

 **Pinwheels**

These little biscuits are perfect for a party.

*Makes about 40*

- ★ 2 ½ cups (18 oz) ready-made puff pastry (thawed if frozen)
- ★ ½ cup strong Cheddar cheese, grated
- ★ 2 tablespoons tomato purée
- ★ pepper and salt

Roll out the pastry on a lightly floured board into a rectangle about ⅕ in thick.

Spread the tomato purée over the pastry and sprinkle the cheese on top.
Add pepper and salt.

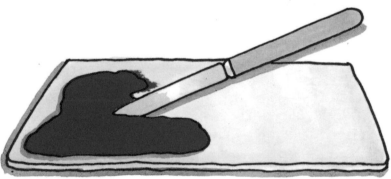

Roll up tightly and wrap in clingfilm. Put in the freezer for about two hours until firm.

Place on a greased baking tray and cook for 10 minutes at 425°F.
Serve warm. Add pepper and salt.

Cut into very thin slices.

## Christmas Biscuits

Use festive-shaped cutters for these. Hang on the tree with red and green ribbons.

*Makes about 20*

- ★ 14 tablespoons (1 ¾ cup) softened butter
- ★ ⅔ cup granulated sugar
- ★ ⅔ cup soft light brown sugar
- ★ 1 egg
- ★ 1 ¾ cup plain flour
- ★ ½ level teaspoon salt
- ★ 1 level teaspoon cinnamon
- ★ 1 level teaspoon ground ginger

Beat the butter and sugars in a large bowl until soft and fluffy. Gradually beat in the egg.

Fold the flour, salt, and spices into the mixture. Beat it well then wrap in clingfilm and chill in the fridge for 30 minutes.

Roll out on a floured surface to roughly ⅕ in thick. Cut out Christmas shapes. Make a hole near the top with the end of a chopstick or similar.

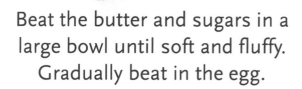

Place the biscuits on greased baking sheets. Prick lightly with a fork. Bake in the oven at 350°F for 12–15 minutes or until light brown.

Cool the biscuits on a wire rack.

# Traditional English Trifle

This is a delicious pudding to make for a special occasion. Make it in a large glass bowl so you can see the pretty, colorful layers.

*For 6 people*

- ★ 6 trifle sponges or plain sponge cake
- ★ raspberry jam
- ★ 1 cup + 2 tablespoons fresh raspberries or large tin raspberries, drained (but keep the juice from the tin)
- ★ ⅕ cup fruit juice or juice from the tin
- ★ 1 ¼ cup + 2 tablespoons custard (see opposite)
- ★ 1 ¼ cup + 2 tablespoons double cream
- ★ ¼ cup toasted flaked almonds

Slice the sponges or cake and spread with some raspberry jam.

Make them into "sandwiches."
Place in the bottom of a large glass bowl.

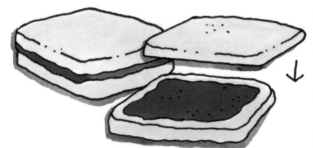

Pour over the fruit juice or juice from the tin, if using. It should all soak into the sponges.

Sprinkle the raspberries on top.

Pour over the custard.
If it is warm leave it to cool.

Whip the cream until it is thick but not stiff. Spoon it carefully over the custard. Smooth the top.

Decorate the top with the almonds. Cool the trifle in the fridge before serving.

## Homemade Custard

- ★ 1 ¼ cup + 2 tablespoons double cream
- ★ 3 egg yolks
- ★ 2 tablespoons (¼ cup) caster sugar
- ★ 1 level teaspoon cornstarch

Heat the cream in a small saucepan. Blend the egg yolks, sugar, and cornstarch in a bowl very thoroughly.

Pour into the hot cream, stirring with a wooden spoon over a very low heat until thick. Do not let it boil.

# Christmas Cards

## Stained Glass Window

★ colored paper 6 in 8 ¼ in ♻
★ old Christmas card ♻
★ pencil and tracing paper
★ glue and scissors

Fold the colored paper in half.

Trace the Stained Glass Window template from page 52. Then trace it on to the Christmas card so it frames a picture. Cut out the window shape.

Cut the pieces out and put them back together with the right side facing up.

Turn it over. Divide it into seven pieces of roughly the same size.

Glue the pieces on to the card leaving a small space between each piece. Leave to dry.

## Snowman

- ★ colored paper 6 in x 8 ¼ in ♻
- ★ white paper ♻
- ★ strip of fabric ♻
- ★ silver glitter
- ★ felt-tip pens
- ★ glue and scissors
- ★ pencil and tracing paper

Fold the colored paper in half. Trace the Snowman template from page 52 on to the white paper. Cut it out and glue it on the front of the card.

Draw the face and details.

Cut the fabric into a strip ¾ in x 6 ¾ in.

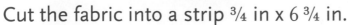

Make a small hole on either side of the snowman's "neck" with the scissors. Push the ends of the fabric through the holes from inside. Knot the ends together. Dab glue around the snowman and down his left side. Sprinkle with glitter.

## Tree Decoration Card

Here a card and gift are combined. After Christmas remove the decoration and hang it on the tree next year.

- ★ stiff colored paper 6 in x 8 ¼ in ♻
- ★ scraps of fabric ♻
- ★ button ♻
- ★ thick card ♻
- ★ yarn or thin string ♻
- ★ needle
- ★ glue
- ★ scissors
- ★ pencil and tracing paper

Trace one of the Tree Decoration Card templates on page 52 on the thick card. Cut it out.

Place on the back of the fabric and draw around it. Cut out two, making them bigger than the outline.

Glue the fabric to both sides of the card shape with the right side of the fabric facing outwards.

Use lots of glue.
If it soaks through it does not matter.
It will dry and not show.

Hold firmly and cut a fine fringe all around the shape close up to it.

*Ruffle the fringe with your fingers and make it fray a bit.*

Thread a 10-in length of yarn or string on to the needle. Push it through the top of the card shape.

Fold the colored paper in half to make a card. Sew the button on to the top center of the card. Wind the loop around the button.

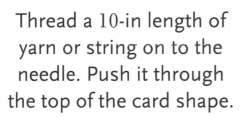

*Pull into even lengths. Knot twice at the top to form a loop.*

## variations

Glue sequins or small buttons on to the decorations.

Use different patterned fabrics for each side.

Use sparkly fabrics or brilliant silks. Tie on to bright, contrasting cards.

**47**

# Gifts Galore

Everyone appreciates something different that has been specially made for them.

## Festive Bookmarks

★ old Christmas cards ♻
★ red yarn ♻
★ ruler and pencil
★ scissors
★ hole punch (optional)

Tear the backs off the cards. Only use cards that have plain backs to the pictures. Cut into strips 2 in x 6 in.

Cut the bottom into a curve or triangle. Make a hole with the hole punch or point of the scissors.

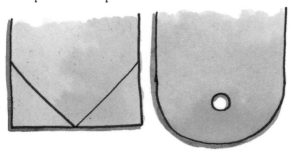

Cut the yarn into three 10-in lengths. Fold in two and push the folded ends through the hole. Then push cut ends through the loop.

Write a message on the back.

# Glasses case

- ★ old wool sweater ♻
- ★ yarn ♻
- ★ button ♻
- ★ needle and thread
- ★ scissors and pins

Put the jumper into a hot wash. This will thicken and felt it. Leave it to dry and then cut a strip measuring 2 ¾ in x 14 in.

Cut one end into a curve or a point. Fold the other end.

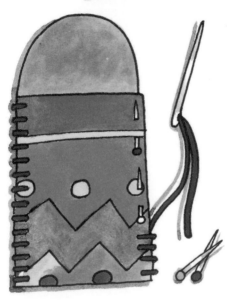

Pin the sides and sew together with yarn.

Sew a yarn loop at the center of the curved edge. Fold over and mark where to put the button. Sew it on.

## Merry Mats

★ 19 metal bottle tops ♻
★ scraps of cotton fabric ♻
★ compass and pencil
★ scissors
★ needle
★ thread

Mark out 19 circles on the fabric.
Use the compass and pencil.
Cut them out.

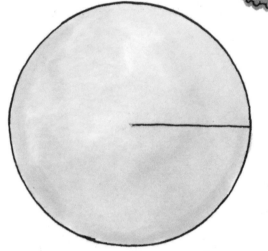

Thread the needle with a double
length of thread. Sew a line of running
stitches around each circle of fabric.

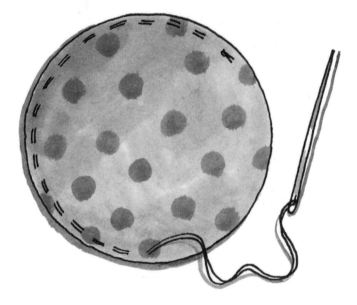

Place the bottle caps face down
on the wrong side of the fabric.
Continue the running stitch to
the end.

Pull the fabric tight around the
bottle tops. Secure it with a few
stitches. Cut off the thread.

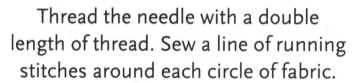
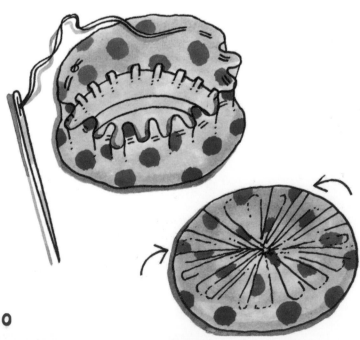

Cover all 19 bottle tops in the same way.
Arrange the tops in a pattern you like.

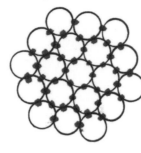

Turn the tops over and start
sewing them together. Begin
with the ones in the center.

Sew a few stitches at the
edges of the tops to join them together.

When they are all sewn turn
the mat over!

## More Mats

Make some smaller and larger mats.

Make a set of four or
six coasters.

Make a large round or oblong serving mat.

# Template Shapes

Look at the instructions on page 4
on how to use these templates

TREE
DECORATION
CARD

SNOWMAN
CARD

CHRISTMAS
CAKE HAT

STAINED GLASS
WINDOW CARD

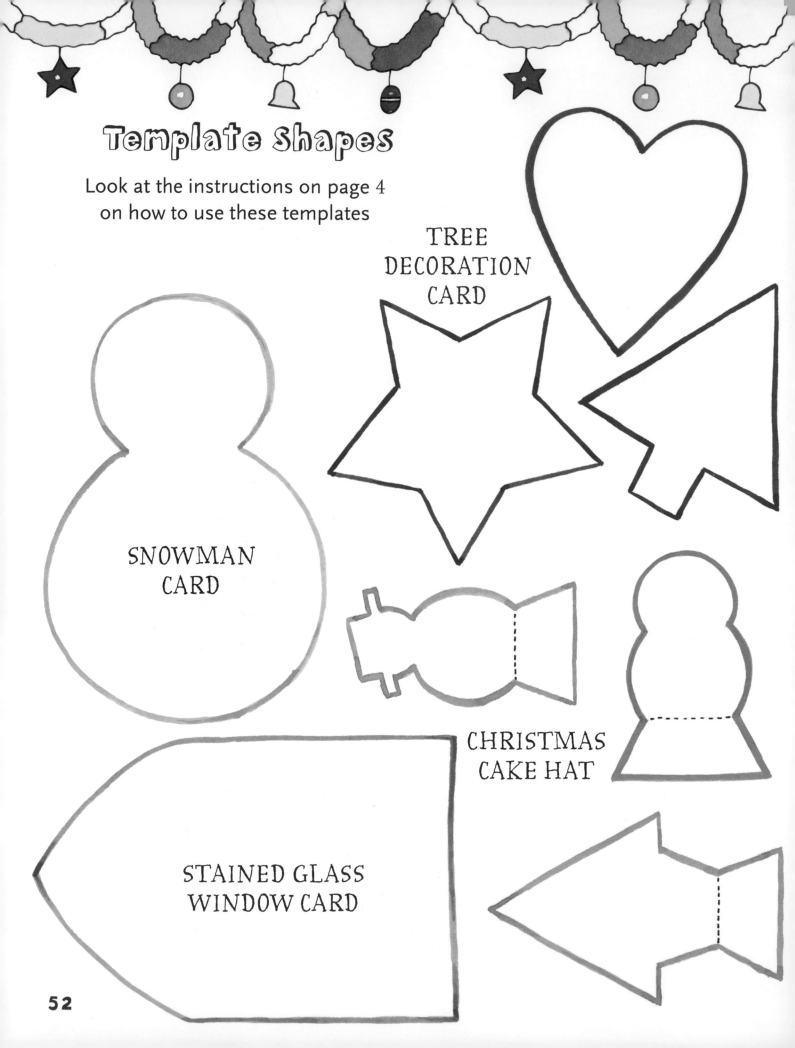

# More colorful Christmas cards and Decorations

# Creative Cards

Here are some more exciting cards you can easily make yourself.
Follow the pictures and simple instructions.

### Shaped cards

When you make shaped cards, it is important to remember to keep one straight piece where you fold the card. This can be either on the left-hand side or the top edge.
Start with a folded square or rectangle of paper or light card. Draw your picture, then cut out the shape.

Fold

Fold

Write your message inside.

Fold

## Window cards

Fold some paper or card in half. Open and cut a shape out of the front. (Use the templates in the back of the book.) Stick patterned paper or paint a picture on the inside. This will then show through the cut-out shape when you close the card.

Decorate with a border around the window shape.

## Cards with hanging cut-outs

Fold some paper or card in half. Open and cut a shape out of the front. Cut out small shapes and hang them from the top of the window on the inside. Use thin thread and sticky tape.

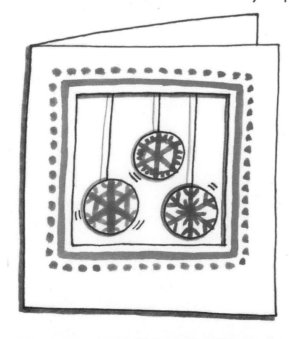

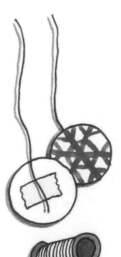

Try different shapes such as snowflakes or stars. Decorate with glitter. Use the template shapes.

## Cards with doors

Cut out a rectangle of paper or card and divide into a central section with two "doors," on either side. Each door should be half the width of the central panel.

Fold the doors to close over the central panel. Draw a surprise inside.

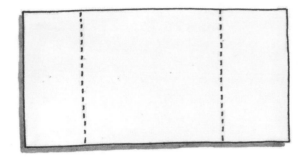

### Ideas for inside
★ curtains and dancer
★ door and party
★ wrapping paper and present

## Nativity card

Add a pointed piece on the top of the central section of the card.

## Pattern cards

Use the templates at the front or back of the book to create shapes you can color in or cover in glitter. Follow the instructions on page 4 to trace the templates.

Draw star shapes on a card. Carefully cover the stars in glue and shake glitter over them.

Merry Christmas

## Gift tags

Use the gift tag templates at the front of the book and the instructions on page 4 to make your own gift tags.

Make a hole at one end and thread yarn, string, or narrow ribbon through.

Dear Granny Merry Christmas love Hannah x x x

Write your message clearly on one side. Decorate the other side.

# Envelopes

Make some colorful envelopes for your cards using the template at the back of the book.

*What you will need:*
- colored paper ♻
- pencil
- tracing paper
- ruler
- scissors
- sticky tape
- glue

**1**

Follow the instructions on page 4 to trace the template on to paper. Cut it out.

**2**

Fold along the dotted lines. Glue the bottom flap on to the two side flaps. Put the card in and glue down the top flap.

Use stickers or small patterns to decorate the envelopes.

You can post your card. Write the name and address clearly and don't forget the stamps!

Jessie

Mr + Mrs J. Thomas,
17, Squirrel Lane,
Oakton,
Hampshire CB4 1QZ

# Nativity scene

Make this simple background to stand behind your Nativity figures from the black and white pages at the end of the book. Cut a strip of cardboard about 8 ¼ x 15 ¾ in. Draw the background picture of the stable and hills. Cut out the shapes along the top.

Be careful with a craft knife.

Score with a craft knife on each side of the stable.

Use the template to make a star from paper. Dab with glue and then add glitter. Stick on the top of the stable.

Paint and leave to dry.

Score and fold.

Score and fold.

Stick smaller sticky stars on the sky. Or use the template to draw and paint them.

Bend gently so the background will stand up.

# Flying dove

Use the dove shape on the template pages at the front of the book. Follow the tracing instructions on page 4 to make this Christmas dove.

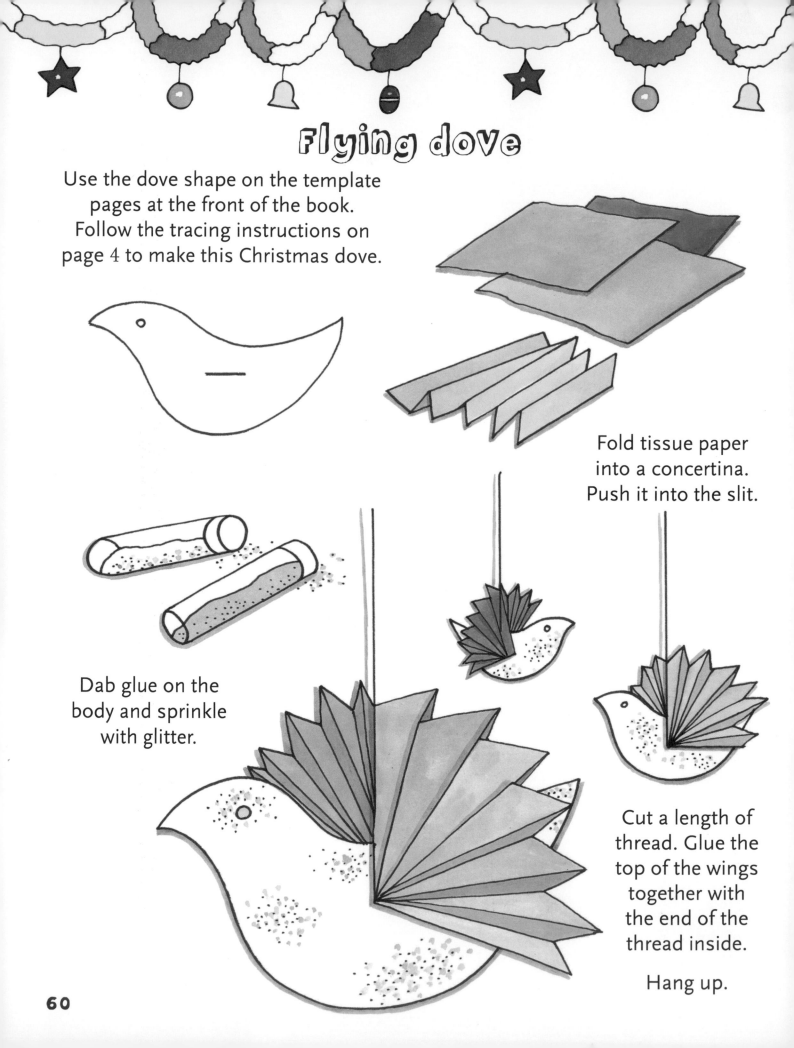

Fold tissue paper into a concertina. Push it into the slit.

Dab glue on the body and sprinkle with glitter.

Cut a length of thread. Glue the top of the wings together with the end of the thread inside.

Hang up.

# Christmas Cone

These look very pretty hanging on the Christmas tree.

Use the template instructions on page 4 and trace the cone and handle outlines below on to colored paper. Use the stencil at the back of the book to decorate with shapes. Or you can use sticky shapes, glue on sequins or draw on patterns with felt-tip pens.

Roll the paper into a cone. Secure with sticky tape. Glue the handle inside at the top.

Put sweets inside.

Cut the curved edge of the cone into different shapes.

scallops

zigzag

fringe

HANDLE TEMPLATE

CONE TEMPLATE

# Napkin rings

Make a set of these Christmas napkin rings for parties or special holiday meals. If you use stiff paper, they can be used several times. Use the template instructions on page 4 to draw this napkin ring shape on to stiff red or white paper. Cut it out. Use the holly leaf templates on the front or back pages of the book to decorate the wreath. Then when it is dry, slot the two ends together to form the ring.

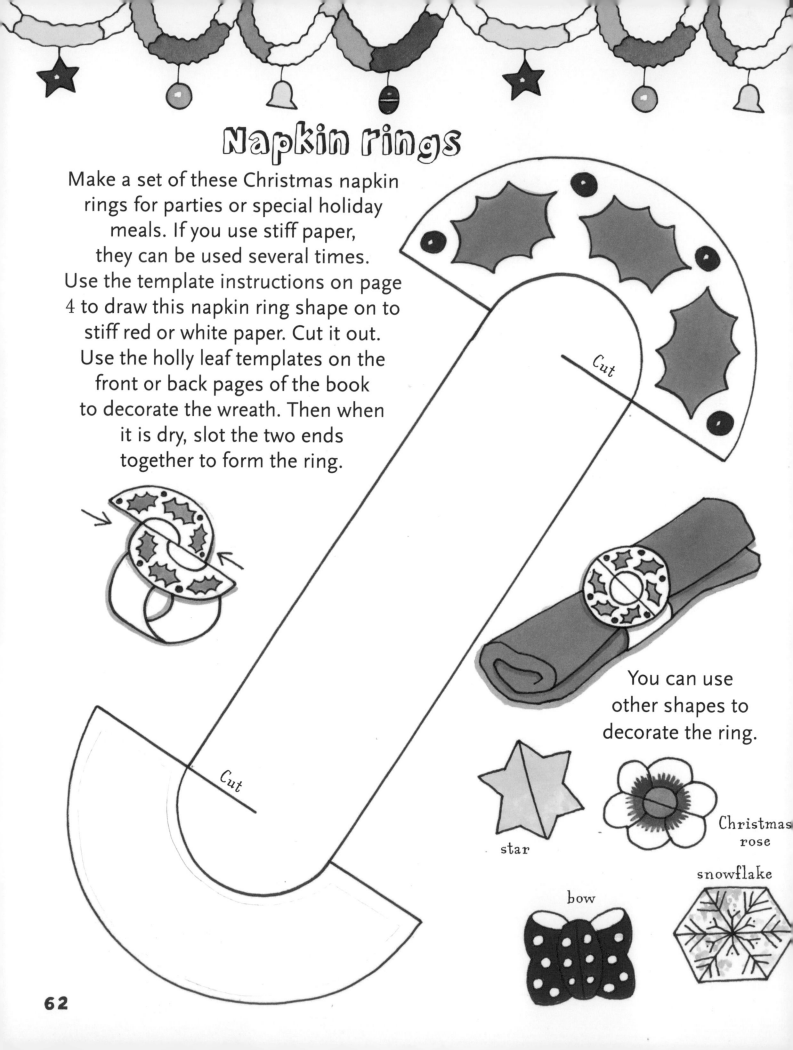

*Cut*

*Cut*

You can use other shapes to decorate the ring.

star

Christmas rose

snowflake

bow

# Christmas streamers

Use the templates on the front and back pages of the book to make these pretty hanging garlands.
Follow the instructions on page 4 and trace some festive shapes on the back of recycled Christmas gift wrap.
Cut them out.

Glue half the shapes on the unpatterned side. Then put them in a row and lay a length of yarn or thin string along the middle. Cover them with the other cut-out and glued shapes.

Hang from a window or around a light shade.

# Cards & Decorations to cut and color

The following pages contain some ready-drawn cards and decorations for you to cut out and color. Cut the pages out of the book before you start. Be careful if you use a craft knife. Then, cut along the solid lines and fold along the dotted lines.

For coloring in, you can use colored pencils, crayons, felt-tip pens, or paints.

Start coloring the center of the cut-outs first. Leave borders until last so you don't smudge them. Leave things flat to dry. Then turn over and color the other side if necessary.

At the back of the book, there is a template that can be used to make envelopes for the cards. Then you can post them to your family and friends.

**Take care when using a craft knife.**

*Some things you will need:*
- ★ crayons, paints and felt-tip pens
- ★ scissors and a craft knife (optional)
- ★ glue
- ★ glitter
- ★ yarn

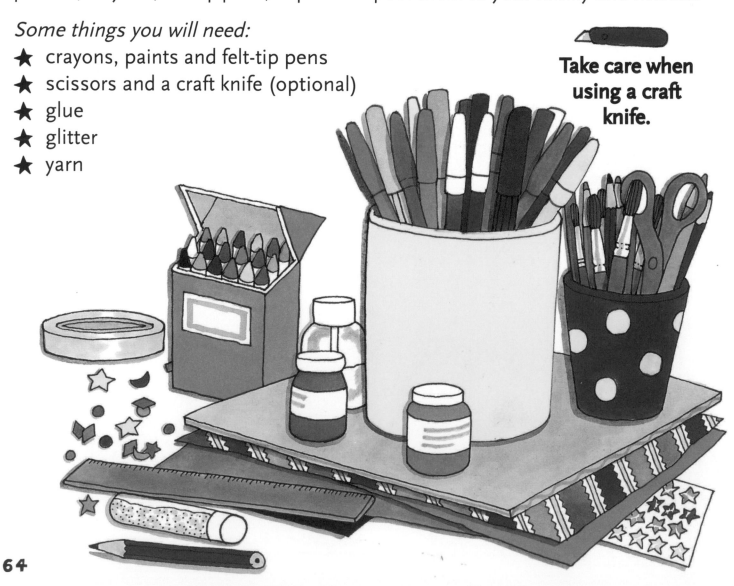

Colored in by

FOLD

FOLD

# Merry Christmas
# and a Happy New Year

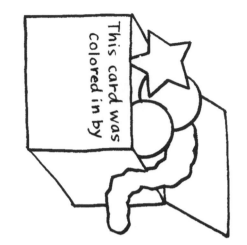

This card was
colored in by

FOLD

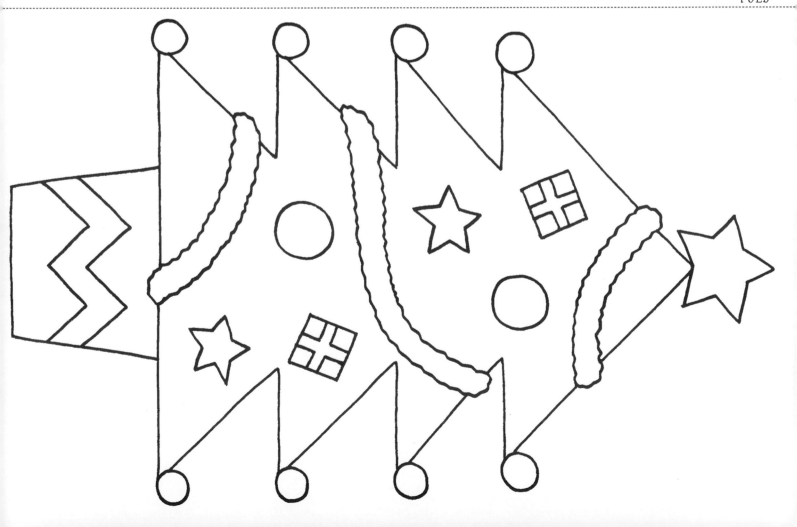

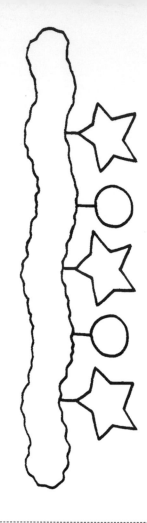

Merry Christmas

FOLD

FOLD

Card colored in by

.........................

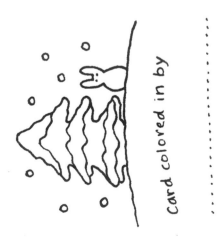

Card colored in by

.........................

CUT

CUT

FOLD

MERRY CHRISTMAS

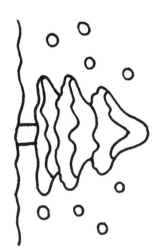

MERRY CHRISTMAS

FOLD

This card was colored in by

This card was colored in by

CUT

CUT

FOLD

MERRY CHRISTMAS

MERRY CHRISTMAS

CUT

Card colored in by

Card coloured in by

FOLD

MERRY
CHRISTMAS

MERRY
CHRISTMAS

Card colored in by

. . . . . . . . . . . . . . . . . . . . . .

CUT

Card colored in by

. . . . . . . . . . . . . . . . . . . . . .

FOLD

CUT

MERRY
CHRISTMAS

MERRY
CHRISTMAS

Colored in by

Merry Christmas

- - - - - - - - - - - - - - - - - - - - - - - - - - - - - - - - - - - - - - - - - - - - - - - - - - - - -

FOLD

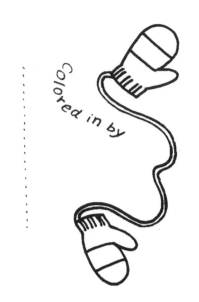

Colored in by

FOLD

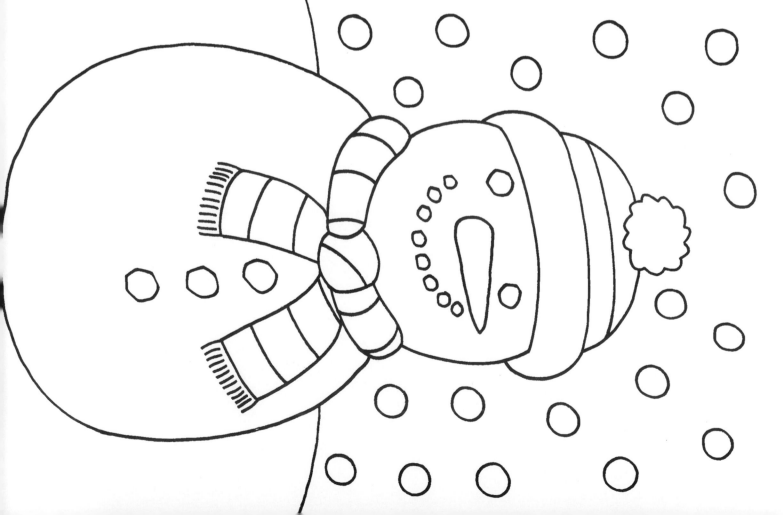

Merry Christmas
and a
Happy New Year

# NATIVITY FIGURES

Color in the figures. Cut out and then fold along the dotted lines. Stand up in front of the Nativity background (see page 59).

Mary

Joseph

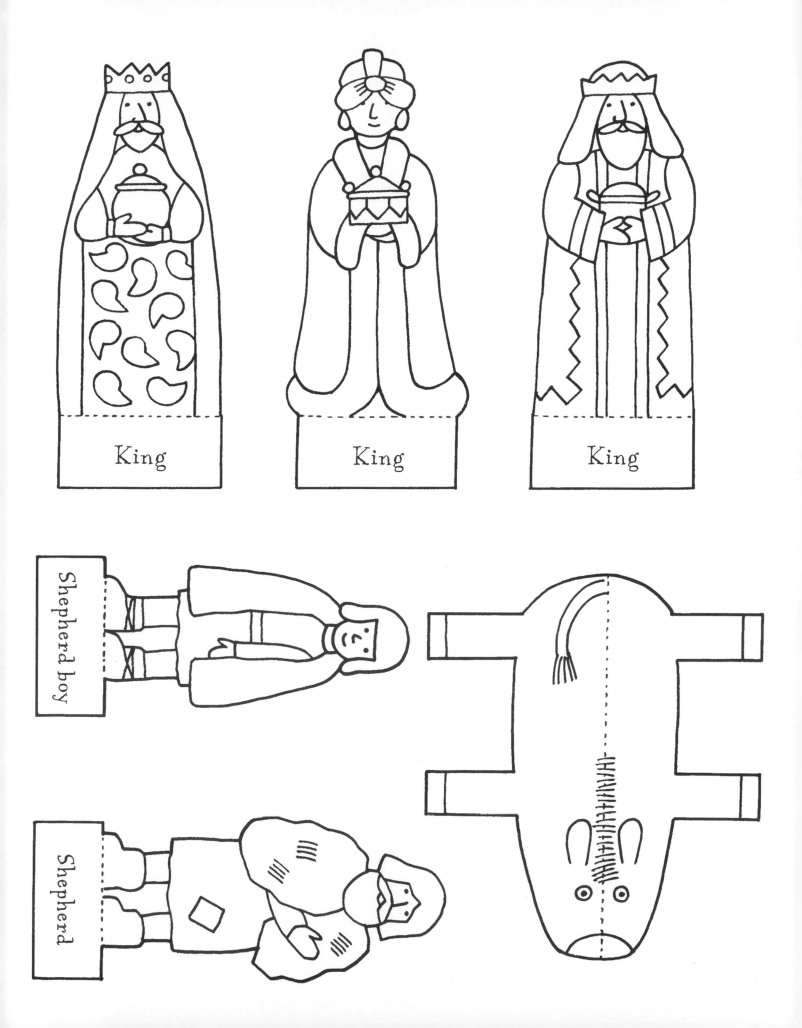

King

King

King

Shepherd boy

Shepherd

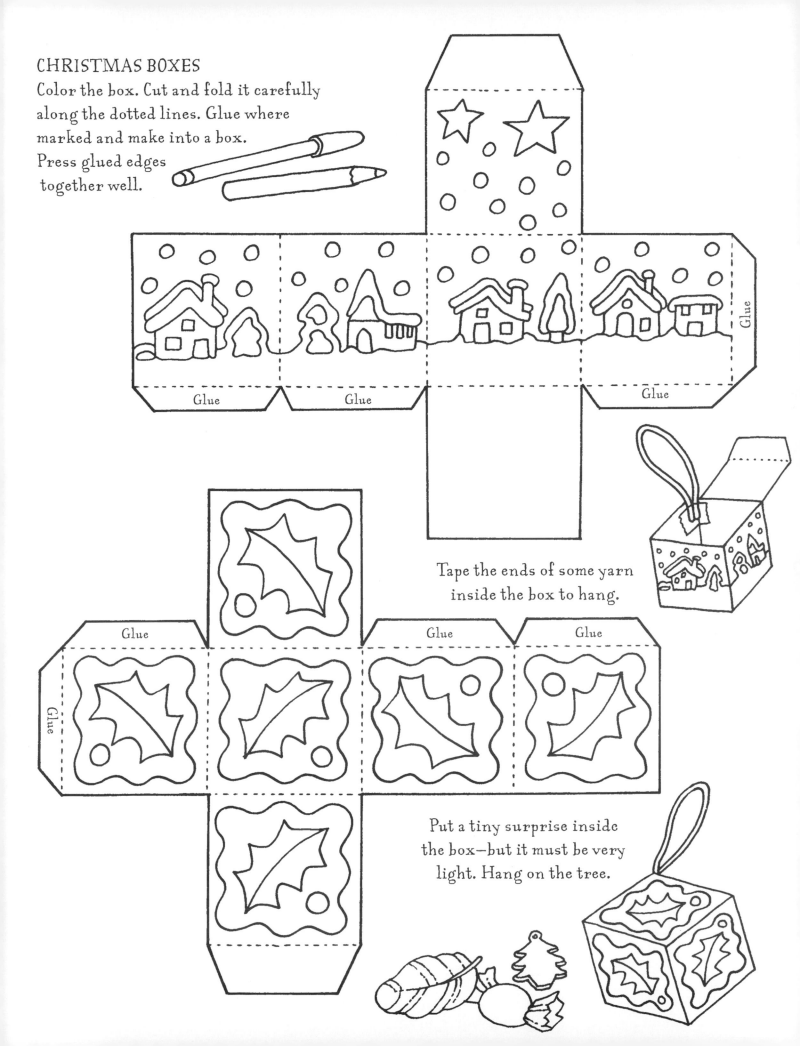

# CHRISTMAS BOXES

Color the box. Cut and fold it carefully along the dotted lines. Glue where marked and make into a box. Press glued edges together well.

Glue

Glue    Glue    Glue

Tape the ends of some yarn inside the box to hang.

Glue    Glue    Glue    Glue

Put a tiny surprise inside the box—but it must be very light. Hang on the tree.

STANDING CARDS
Color in and decorate both sides
of the cards. Cut out. Cut along the line
down the center of the cards.
Slot together.

# SNOWFLAKES

Dab glue on to the snowflakes and sprinkle glitter on both sides. Cut out and cut down one line to the center of each snowflake. Slot together.

Glue the end of yarn or string to the top of the snowflake and hang up.

**CHRISTMAS ANGEL and FAIRY**
Color the figures or decorate them with glue and glitter.

Cut them out including the arms. Curl the arms forward by pulling carefully along closed scissors.

Pull the skirt around to form cone and secure with sticky tape on the inside.

# CHRISTMAS LANTERNS

Color them and cut them out.
Fold in two lengthways. Cut
along the lines with scissors.

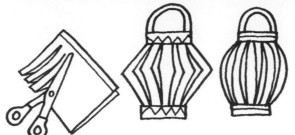

Pull together and tape
the top and bottom.
Tape handle inside the
top and hang up.

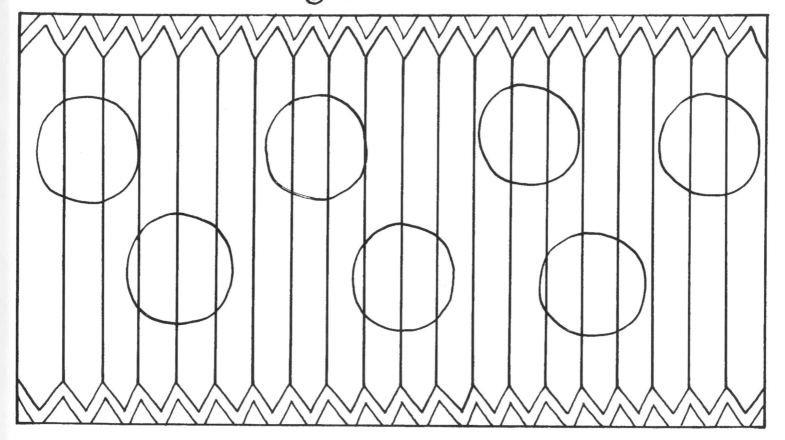

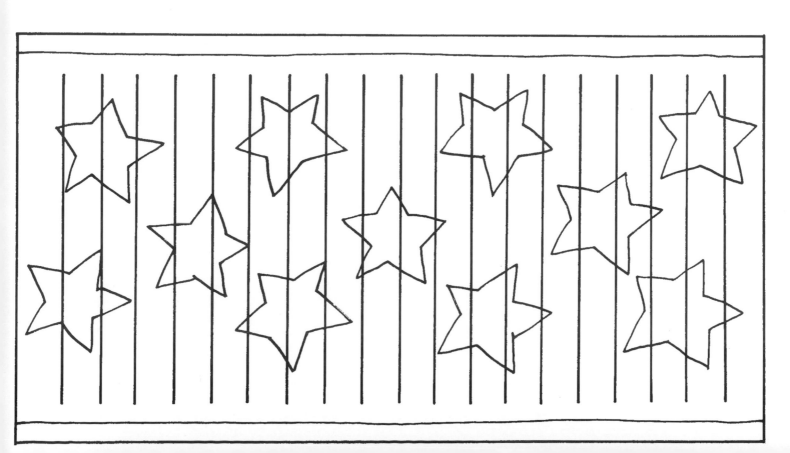

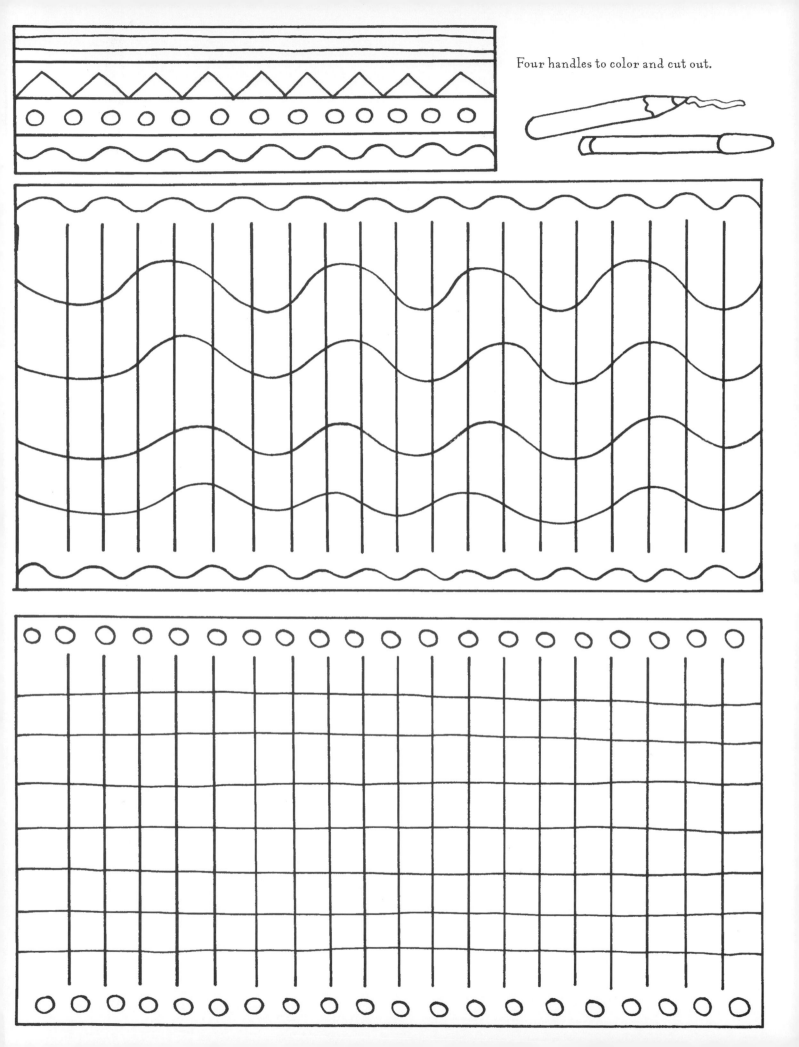

Four handles to color and cut out.

Father Christmas has come but everyone else is still asleep.
Color in and decorate your Christmas tree.